THOUGHT CATALOG BOOKS

To My Fellow Women

To My Fellow Women

THOUGHT CATALOG

THOUGHT CATALOG BOOKS

Brooklyn, NY

Contents

1. To My Fellow Women, Please Don't Settle   1
    —*Marisa Donnelly*

2. To My Fellow Women, This Is How You Deserve To Be   5
    Treated
    —*Kirsten Corley*

3. Sweet Girl, You Are Whole Without Him   9
    —*Kim Quindlen*

4. To My Fellow Women, Prince Charming Isn't Going To   13
    Save You
    —*Lauren Jarvis-Gibson*

5. To Every Girl Who Is Tired Of Being Told 'I'm Not   17
    Looking For Something Serious'
    —*Nicole Tarkoff*

6. For The Women Who Feel Like 'Too Much'   21
    —*Heidi Priebe*

7. Dear Woman, You Can Be Whatever You Want To Be   25
    —*Margioleh G. Alonzo*

8. To All The Girls Who Are Terrified Of Love   29
    —*Lauren Jarvis-Gibson*

9. My Fellow Women, Please Don't Give Up On Love   33
    —*Zoe Jones*

10. Sweet Girl, Allowing Yourself To Love Again Is The   37
    Bravest Thing You Can Do
    —*Lacey Ramburger*

11. Be The Girl Who Can Love Unapologetically, Even After   41
    Her Heart Breaks
    —*Becca Martin*

12. Please, Be This Kind Of Woman   45
    —*Marisa Donnelly*

13. All Women Are 'Real' Women   49
    —*Rachel Yang*

14. What A Real Woman Looks Like   53
    —*Ari Eastman*

15. To My Fellow Women: Be Whatever The Fuck You Want   55
    —*Kendra Syrdal*

16. To The Girls Who Need To Know They Deserve Better   59
    —*Sierra Poston*

1

To My Fellow Women, Please Don't Settle

Marisa Donnelly

Not in a job you hate, not in a town where you don't feel at home, not with friendships that aren't real, and especially, *especially* not with love.

You deserve someone who will smile at your silly jokes, who will kiss your forehead when you've had a long day, and who will absentmindedly reach for your hand across the center console when he's driving, just because he wants to feel your fingers twisted with his.

You deserve a guy who doesn't just spend the night, but spends the morning. Who cooks your favorite chocolate chip waffles with peanut butter and brings them on a tray to your bed when you're sick. Who hums your favorite song, off-key and awkward, just to make you laugh. Who takes you on a walk to his favorite hill in town, and kisses you as the sun sets.

You are strong and gentle, determined and loving, complicated and kind, and you deserve someone who looks past your flaws and the way you curl your hair, and sees your beautiful *heart*.

So please, my sister, don't settle. Don't settle for the man who texts you at three in the morning, or only when you're at a party without him, or only when you're happy with someone else.

Don't settle for the boy who plays mind games, who calls you hurtful names, who spins you around in his lies until you're so dizzy and tired you just give in.

Don't settle for the guy who sees only a face, only a body, because sweet girl, you will always be more than a body.

I know you might feel lost right now. You might be scared. You might be terrified of being lonely. And you might be thinking *this is it, this is all there is.* But I promise you, there's so much more.

There will be a man whose fingers will trace the freckles on your cheeks and send goosebumps down your back. Whose arms will hold you during the fireworks on the fourth of July. Whose lips will taste like your Mike's Hard Lemonade because he won't stop kissing you. Whose smile will make your head spin like you're drunk, but even better.

There will be a man who will answer your calls, who will take you on dates, who will, despite the distance and despite the childish boys of your past, truly *love you, choose you.* Every. Single. Day.

So please promise me this: That you will hold out for him. That you won't settle for the cheapened version of love. That you won't kiss away the unsatisfied taste on your

tongue. That you won't go to bed next to someone else, wishing for more.

There will be more. So much more.

Don't settle for anything less than excitement and jumping beans in the pit of your stomach. Nothing less than forever. Nothing less than *knowing,* beyond a doubt that this is love.

Because I promise, you'll find it. And it will be more beautiful than you ever imagined.

2

To My Fellow Women, This Is How You Deserve To Be Treated

Kirsten Corley

Somewhere along the way, we've all become guilty of accepting much less than we deserve. And instead of this standard we once had that was so high, we find flattery in not being treated like shit. We've allowed immediate gratification, to screw with our heads. We've accepted way less than we've deserved. We've allowed people to talk to us, in a manner that's demeaning. And as long as they say sorry after we cry, we forgive them. We've succumb to peer pressure and pleasing others without asking someone for something we want. We've been made to feel guilty for even asking. Because somewhere along the way someone has told us we don't deserve that, and we foolishly believed them.

But I'm here to tell you, you never deserved any of those things. Because the things you want are out there, and the person who will treat you well and with respect is wondering where all the people who deserve it are. We've allowed ourselves to alter our perception, of what we are looking for and it's messing with us.

But you shouldn't settle for average or mediocre.

Because you deserve more than that. Because I know exactly what you'd be willing to give someone else, and that's what you deserve.

You deserve every fantasy to become reality. You deserve those cliches you watch in movies, to come to reality before your eyes and not just on a screen.

You deserve someone asking you to slow dance on a week-night in the street.

You deserve someone unapologetically pouring their heart out to you. Not just you being the one to say I love you and someone reply thank you.

You deserve a radio being played outside your window. Not songs that make you cry as you find the company in heartbreak.

You deserve flowers sent to your office. But if he knows you, he'll know to send chocolate first.

You deserve being a part of their entire world, not being their best-kept secret.

You deserve Sunday morning where they want you to stay.

You deserve to never feel badly for saying what you think and feel.

You deserve texts to always be answered fast. And not leave you confused.

You deserve actual phone calls because he's had a bad day and just hearing your voice make it better.

You deserve someone who wants to be there, not someone who is bored.

You deserve sleeping next to someone who leaves you whole, not lying next to a stranger that makes you feel lonely.

You deserve long car rides where you don't know where you are going, but there's a confidence in the person next to you, because no matter where that might be, you'll get there together.

You deserve someone singing you your favorite song, even if it took them weeks to learn.

You deserve someone who wants to go to the ends of the earth to be with you, not someone who makes you go all the way alone.

Because relationships are 50/50.

You deserve kissing without asking. Because they want to.

And making love, not just having sex. Because there is a difference between sleeping with someone and doing it with someone you love.

You deserve to have someone helps carry the burdens life

throws at you. Because life struggles were never meant to be endured alone. You don't deserve someone who is making things more complicated.

You deserve someone drying your tears, never causing them.

You deserve all these things. You just have to be brave enough to ask for it. Because it's there, you're vision though has been made blurry with tears.

Please, my dear, life is too short and you are too young, you are too beautiful, you are too worth it to settle for anything less than extraordinary. And I know you question if it's out there, but it is. It's waiting for you, but you are fixating upon these men or boys that are temporary highs. That's all they will ever be. But when you meet the right person that temporary high you get addicted to, will last your entire life.

Because soul mates are real. And love is something you can believe in. I need you to trust. Trust it blindly until it becomes a reality.

3

Sweet Girl, You Are Whole Without Him

Kim Quindlen

Maybe he broke your heart, maybe he didn't. Maybe he wanted you, maybe he didn't. Maybe he's still yours, maybe he's long gone. Maybe he was jerk, maybe he is the greatest guy you've ever met. Maybe you're married, maybe you're single. Maybe you're in the healthiest relationship you've ever been in, or maybe you've never been more confused in your life.

The situation doesn't matter. Your heart could be full or broken, steady or shaken. Pieced back together, or shattered all across the memories of him you've been forced to leave behind. No matter what happened to you then, no matter what's happening to you now. No matter how happy or how sad you are, or how confident or how lost you feel—you are whole without him. You are a being all on your own, a light, a presence, an existence. You are a strong soul, no matter how broken you may feel. You are you, completely, regardless of where he fits or used to fit into your life. You are a combination of all the lessons you've learned, all the feelings you've felt, all the choices you've made, all the things you've said, all of the battles you've fought, all the love you've given and received.

And being with him, or not being with him, will never take any of that away from you.

You are whole without him, you are person outside of his existence. You always have been and you always will be. Maybe it doesn't always feel that way. Maybe sometimes you feel like you've lost yourself because of him, or you've lost yourself within him. But you haven't. You're always there, you're always you. Sometimes it just takes a little longer to pull yourself out, especially if you've been shattered before. The instinct can be to hide, to close in on yourself in order to survive. To allow yourself to camouflage into your surroundings, in order to protect your heart—even if you're with someone who you know will take care of it. But regardless of how far away your true self feels to you, you're always there, somewhere. You just have to remember to look, to remember you are whole and that you can find yourself on your own.

Knowing that you are whole—and that you are whole without him—doesn't make you hard, or callous, or too rough around the edges. It doesn't make you a man-hater, a bitch, a cold-hearted ice queen. It doesn't mean you view all men as evil and wrong. It doesn't mean you're stubborn or trying to prove anything. There is nothing here to apologize for. There is nothing weird about wanting to be, and believing that you are, a full and complete person outside of him. He can or could have been part of you—part of the things you've felt and experienced and learned. It doesn't invalidate who he was or who he still is to you. It just means that even without him, still, there is so much to you. That outside of your relationship with him or your breakup with him or whatever else he is to you, that you are still your own person, your own self—with a history, a point of view, a set of beliefs and a set of values, things you want, goals for the future, things you've accomplished and things you've failed at, people you love and people who love you.

You are your own protagonist, not a supporting character in someone else's story.

Some people might make you feel weird, for being so self-assured. They might accuse you of just being angry, bitter, scorned. But figuring out, or wanting to figure out, who you are outside of another person does not make you hate-filled or resentful. If your heart was broken, then sure, you're probably holding onto some anger and sadness. But overall, making the choice to get to know yourself really has nothing to do with him. It *could* mean that you're working through some pain, but it's just as normal to be in a happy, healthy relationship and still have a strong desire to solidify who you are outside of him.

It is not about hate, resentment, revenge. It's not about him at all. It's about the empowerment of you, the joy of getting to know yourself, the wonder of setting yourself free—and discovering that, in the process, all it does it make your heart even bigger, and even more open to love. You're out there, somewhere, you just have to look. Do it for you.

4

To My Fellow Women, Prince Charming Isn't Going To Save You

Lauren Jarvis-Gibson

Growing up, I watched Snow White being revived just from a simple kiss. I watched Sleeping Beauty being saved just by a prince's kiss. And then I watched Ariel almost kill herself just to be with a man she had never met before.

Those movies ultimately showed me that these women were never going to be truly happy without their Prince Charming. They wouldn't even be alive without a precious kiss from them. I never thought I would be just like them, but as it turns out, my subconscious thought differently. I'm not going to blame childhood movies for wanting my own Prince Charming, but I think we all do want our own happy ending, and we want it standing by someone else.

I thought I met my Prince Charming when I was seventeen. And I guess I did for a while. He saved me from my own demons, from my negative thoughts, from my insults to my own self. He made me feel like I was the most beautiful thing on this earth. And I ate it up. I thought that he was all I needed to be happy.

But, after a while you realize that this person can't save you from yourself. You have to do it alone. And eventually, you'll realize that you won't need a boy to stand beside you. You'll just need you.

I could probably write a thousand more articles on the loss of who I thought was my "Prince Charming," but that's not the point of this article. The point of this is that whether you have lost the love of your life, or whether you have been single for so long that you've forgotten what it's like to have loved, it's happening for a reason. And I know, it feels like your heart will never recover. It feels like you could truly die from a broken heart. And you feel like a ghost of your past self, like you don't even know yourself anymore.

And that's because you don't. **Maybe this is all a sign from the universe that you need to focus on yourself, learn to be by yourself and to adore yourself. It's a sign that you need to be your own damn person.** And you need to love yourself in order to eventually be loved back. Then, you won't need his kiss to hang on to. You won't need his touch in order to breathe. You won't need his whispers to calm your fast beating heart. You won't need his love to save you. No matter how lonely or awful you feel, no man will ever fix you like you think he will. Your demons will always come back to you when he leaves.

You are stronger than you think. And I promise, you are better off hurting alone then hurting secretly along side another person. F*** Ariel and her desperation for Prince Eric that nearly destroyed her. F*** Sleeping Beauty needing to be saved by a prince who probably had nothing better to offer to her than a few lip locks.

F*** the notion that you need another human being to be your savior. You have your own precious and beautiful self. I promise you, that's all you need. You just need you.

5

To Every Girl Who Is Tired Of Being Told 'I'm Not Looking For Something Serious'

Nicole Tarkoff

I know that you feel like you're not good enough. Not good enough for someone to commit to you fully, to commit to you *only*. Not good enough to receive the same love your heart is capable of giving, not good enough to receive any love at all. You feel this way because he told you he wasn't looking for something serious.

So what was he looking for? What did he think *you* were looking for?

Did he think you'd smile and nod your head? *It's okay to fuck me and never talk to me again.*

Did he think you'd politely go along? *I'm not looking for anything serious, either.*

Did you think you could change his mind? *You couldn't.*

You never wanted to love someone who didn't love you back, but unrequited love is often the kind that teaches us the most about ourselves, because the love that he doesn't give you, you have to give back to yourself.

You can sit and wonder why. Wonder what you don't have that meets the criteria for 'serious.' If you're not something serious, what are you? A mere moment in his timeline? Another face he'll remember but name he'll forget? *What am I?* you wonder. *Hopeless*, you respond.

You can sit and wonder *when*. When *will* he be looking for something serious? How long will you have to wait or are you waiting for nothing?

You can sit and wonder *who*. Who will make him want something serious? Will it be you?

When he tells you this don't wonder. Don't ask why, when, or who. Instead have the confidence to understand what it is *you* want. Not from him, but from life, from love, from this constantly changing universe you find yourself in. Have the invincibility to realize that there's something more important than being his 'something serious.' Have the strength to be yourself, and to never change for someone else. Don't try to be his 'something' because who you already are is so much more than that.

I'm not looking for something serious translates to *I will never love you the way you wish to be loved*, and he didn't. But just because he wasn't looking for something serious, doesn't mean you won't find someone who is. And it sure as hell doesn't mean you don't *deserve* someone who is.

You won't mean *something* to *someone*, you will mean *everything* to one person. You'll find them, and they won't tell you they're not looking for something serious. They'll tell you that they've been looking for someone like you for a very long time. And you will feel the same exact way. You will feel loved like you deserve to feel loved.

6

For The Women Who Feel Like 'Too Much'

Heidi Priebe

For the women who feel like 'too much'—you know exactly who you are.

You're the ones who grew up always feeling different—feeling crazy, feeling brash, feeling just a little too passionate and fierce. You're the ones who've spent your whole lives being told to bite your tongue, to sit on your hands, to settle down and shut up and quell your restless mind for just long enough to blend in.

To find your place within the calmer, cooler crowds.

You're the ones who've always struggled to regulate your spirit. The ones who've felt the pull between the wild and the tame—the never-ending yearning to go and yet the underlying longing to stay. The constant need to explore further and yet the quiet desire to settle down.

You're the ones who can't find peace within yourself. Who have always wanted to try harder, run faster, push yourself further than the world around you ever expected you to go.

You're the ones with the expectations so high that even you can never live up to yourself. Even you can sometimes find your mind to be 'too much' for your body.

And yet you're also the one who's irreplaceable.

You're the one who may always be a little too passionate, a little too reckless and too intense.

But you're also the one who loves the hardest. Who fights the longest. Who refuses to cash in her chips and give up when the rest of the crowd has laid their swords down and gone home.

You're the one who keeps pushing for the changes that need making. Who won't sit down or shut up or settle down when what the stakes are rising higher than you're ready for. You're the one who's not afraid to stand up when the rest of the world is staying silent.

You're the one who may always be 'too much' for the people who are calm and complacent and steady.

But you'll never be too much for the fierce ones.

You'll never be too much for the ones who burn as brightly, who reel as wildly, who move as quickly as you.

You'll never be too much for the people who want to experience the whole of life fully—arms wide open and spirit braced for whatever's coming their way. You will always be *just the right amount* for the people who's fire matches your own.

But there's a catch-22 when it comes to finding them.

Because they're not the ones sitting down. Shutting up. And listening to what they have been told their entire life to do.

They are the ones running ahead of the pack.

And if it's not too much for you to handle, it is up to you to run and catch up.

7

Dear Woman, You Can Be Whatever You Want To Be

Margioleh G. Alonzo

Be reckless. Continue playing with fire because you are the match that this world badly needs to be alive. Continue flirting with the passion that burns inside your heart so that your environment will wonder how you keep your optimism inside this insane and chaotic world we live in. Continue searching for the secrets you hide for fear that the world will not accept you for your flaws and weaknesses.

Be insane. Braid your hair with bubble gum, wash it, and change its color to blue. Wear long skirts and long shirts and long earrings. Mix that red lipstick of yours with orange eye shadow and brown eyeliner pencil. Wear those huge brown shoes you hide at your cabinet because someone told you those shoes don't fit. Continue writing your crush's name at the back of your hand, at the back of your neck, or on the back of your bedroom door. Doodle on your face and add stars to your drawing; color your face with red and orange and violet pens and post your illustration on your bedroom door and scribble these words: "You are colorful, you are not made up of stars because…You. Are. The. Star."

Be a risk-taker. Learn that dance you've been dying to perform. Join an organization. Be the class president or your college's president or your university's president. Say "No" and state your argument. Search how to bake that cake even if you do not know which is the baking soda and which is the flour. Learn how to bike and be happy when you stumble at the end of the road. Woman, be proud of your mistakes because those wounds are your trophy of bravery. Sing wholeheartedly not only inside the bathroom but also inside the library, in the market, inside a moving bus, beside a professor, beside your #1 enemy, on a bridge, inside a coffee shop, and ignore if someone scratches his or her head because of your voice. Listen, your voice is unique and beautiful and no other person in the world has the same voice like you. Some day they will be thankful that they heard you singing and they watched you being carefree amidst the pessimism and inhibitions of this world. Make your hair short; cut it if you want. At the end of the day, you are the lone creator of your happiness.

Be brave. Stand and speak. Do not make someone's statement about how 'bossy' or how 'boastful' or how 'foolish' you are stop you from being the woman you wanted to be. Do not make them feel that they win and achieve their goal of putting you down, their goal of putting you at the margins or even at the back of the margins and their goal of letting you feel that you are an inferior kind of individual. You are never an inferior one. Stand and speak. Protect the right that our suffragettes won for us. Be involved in political and electoral affairs. Do not be afraid of the differing opinions that you will encounter; instead, be excited because you get the chance to display that you are a woman with intense bravery. Dear woman, being brave is also being beautiful. Slay them with your words. Leave them gasping. Leave them clapping for you.

But, dear woman, do not just be reckless; be insane, be a risk-taker, or be brave. **Be everything.** Do not be sad that you still haven't heard the words 'You are pretty' because pretty is just a six-letter word and it will never ever ever ever define who you are. You are more than pretty. You are made of blood and fire and ice and storms and thunder and words. That is why some people are afraid to touch you because you are a masterpiece. I repeat, you are a living and breathing masterpiece. Our ancestors offered their lives so that they could create a world where a woman would be accepted, appreciated, and heard.

Yes, you still have many battles to fight in this patriarchal society, but the reality that you could be everything you wanted to be is a blessing you have to embrace. Be everything. Be amazing. Be intelligent. Be cool. Be awesome. Be a fighter. Be a dancer. Be a singer. Be a writer. Or be a dancer and singer and writer at the same time. Be a nurse. Be an athlete. Conquer the world of sports. Be a leader. Conquer the world of politics. Be a scientist. Conquer the world of science, technology, engineering, and math. Be an astronaut. Be an activist. Be a speaker. Be a fighter.

Be everything. Be a woman. Be you.

8

To All The Girls Who Are Terrified Of Love

Lauren Jarvis-Gibson

Sweet girl, I know you're scared to open up your heart to a foreign one you've never seen or felt before. And I understand that completely. It seems crazy to jump head first into something that could possibly end. It seems like it would just be easier to forget that you even feel something in the first place. Maybe if you could ignore your feelings, then you wouldn't have to go through the beautiful mess that we all call love.

But, that's just the thing. Love is not just a mess. It's a beautiful, gorgeous, life changing mess. It can be dirty, yes, and it also can be detrimental. But, it is *worth* it. No matter what. Every single time. Regardless of whether the story ends up broken or alive, it is so worth it.

Every single person who you have loved before has taught you important lessons about what you want and what you don't want. And that's just a tiny part of your journey. Life is going to surprise you, I promise. And it might be five years from now or twenty years from now, but eventually you are going to find the partner that fits all of those things that you wanted all along.

Closing yourself up to love right now will not do you any good. It won't save you from ever being hurt or ever being broken. It will do nothing but hurt you in the long run.

So, here's what you need to do.

When you feel those butterfly wings start to flutter in your stomach, listen.

And when your hands start to sweat whenever you see the person you like, listen. When you find yourself stuttering like an incompetent middle schooler, listen. Please listen to what your body is saying and go do something about it.

So many times, I have hidden in fear. I have been scared of rejection. I've tried ignoring what my heart was telling me. And I've ignored what my body was telling me. But there is absolutely no reason to ignore those butterflies, that racing heart beat and those sweaty palms. Embrace it. Don't run the opposite direction, sweet girl. You'll regret it if you do.

I've only experienced love once. And even though I got hurt in the end, I still will never regret meeting him and sharing my world with him. I'll never regret the nights we spent star gazing, the days we spent with intertwined fingers, and the years we spent loving one another. I will never regret a single day that I got to share with him.

Because it's the closest thing to perfect that I've ever felt.

And it was the closest thing to magic that I've ever been a part of.

You will get hurt in your lifetime. And when it happens, you are not going to want go on anymore. You're going to want to give up. But sweet girl, *love* is the only thing that won't let you give up. And love is the only thing that will make you get up on some mornings. Because it's all we as human beings want. And it's what we will eventually get.

It's normal to be terrified of love. Everyone on this earth is. But, don't let that fear dictate you. You deserve to experience all the magic in the world that love will give you. You deserve to kiss someone and hear their heartbeat race just like yours. You deserve the kind of love that makes you believe that good things do happen. And you deserve to know what love feels like in every crevasse of your body.

Sweet soul, your heart deserves to be held. And your heart deserves to be adored.

9

My Fellow Women, Please Don't Give Up On Love

Zoe Jones

I know that it is difficult to navigate the pitfalls of hook-up culture. It feels like this exciting world of low consequence—physical relationships have it out for us. We're damned if we do, and damned if we don't.

It is our enemy and our friend. It is the thing that allows us to bring a guy home, and not talk about it the next morning. But, it's also the thing that makes us not want to look this person in the eyes the next day when we see him. And this is not from fear of judgment from others, it is from fear of connecting.

It's the thing that makes us terrified of the word dating, and scoff at the concept of relationships.

We overthink it all. The texts, the glances, the time we spend with someone is all carefully calculated using some algorithm that figures out just the right amount of interest to show. God forbid we show too much interest, it's akin to a death sentence for the casual nature of "hanging out." And it is never a "date," but always "hanging out."

Well girls, I too, am guilty of this. I am scared of commitment. I am scared of being let down by the realities of a relationship, and the preconceived notions I have of it all being proven untrue. I have an idyllic fantasy of dating, one that tells me I should be head over heels for a person before making any type of commitment.

But in reality, it is not as earth-shattering as it seems. I mean, yes, you are creating an attachment to this person, but it's just a concept, a title. That is why the word boyfriend ends in "friend," because first and foremost, he is just your friend.

Many of us share these same frustrations, and most of us just accept them at face value. We think that it just has to be the way that it is. Well, maybe we should stop shying away from commitment, especially if it is something that you find yourself craving. Maybe we need to give it a shot.

Yes, I do realize that dating is not a reality for everyone, given jobs, school, and all of the rest. But if you can, and want to, you should do it. If you meet someone that you relate to in a romantic sense, and the opportunity is there, you should take it.

Maybe all of us should dive headfirst into feeling for others, even considering the risk of being hurt that it poses to us.

Because at the core of vulnerability for another human being is potential. Potential for feelings and connections that would otherwise never have been found. And that's what our college years are centered around: **potential.**

<u>10</u>

Sweet Girl, Allowing Yourself To Love Again Is The Bravest Thing You Can Do

Lacey Ramburger

Oh darling, please allow yourself to love again.

I know it's terrifying. I know that in your head all you can see are the ways it can go wrong. How it *will* go wrong. I understand that you've already done this whole "love" thing, and it left you shattered and so scattered in the wake that you just can't imagine going through it again. You don't want to get your hopes up because you don't want to be let down again. I've been there, so believe me that when I say this it's not because I think you should just get over it and move on. I'm saying it because love is the best possible thing we posses in our lives, and it would be tragic for you to never open yourself up again.

I know you're not ready right now, and that's okay. You need to heal, and you need to relearn how to love again. Yet love isn't simply restrained to romantic partners.

In fact, I think the only way you can ever truly learn to love someone again is to look around at all the types of love surrounding you now.

Once you finally start to grasp the different types of love flowing all around you, you begin to realize just how much love is truly worth it in the end. You realize that even now, you already love and are loved by people. You're afraid of something that is already threading its way through your life even if it's in the subtlest ways. I know that romantic love seems different from the kind of love you have with others, but when you really look at it, it's not that different at all.

Look around you. You have friends who are there for you every day and love you regardless of if you're in your best clothes or in your sweatpants with those three holes in it. Their love is consistent, and they are there when you need a shoulder to cry on as well as someone to laugh with. **Learn to love them in the ways they love you—in the ways they love your mind and your personality, not your body.** When you learn to love people who love your mind, you learn to love the way you think and experience things too.

You also have family/people like family who love you so unconditionally you can't understand it sometimes. They love you despite every crazy, ridiculous, and oftentimes stupid thing you do. Even when you're in the wrong, they still love you at the end of it all. Learn to accept that love because once you realize that someone is capable of loving you despite all of your flaws, you start to understand that the ones before who walked away didn't truly love you.

And then, you have yourself. Look at yourself, darling, I know that you are your own worst critic. You know every good and bad thing about you better than most. Yet look at all you've done in your life, and you're still here. You survived and lived another day. You know there are good things that you bring to this world—you exist in this world and it's better because you're in it.

When you love yourself and the strength you posses in that lion heart of yours, you begin to see the worth you've held all along that others tried to take from you.

Love is the thing we live for, die for, and fight for. We can't always explain it, and we aren't always good at it, but we crave it none the less. We were made to love and be loved. **Don't let the one who broke you keep you broken.** Because one day, you will find someone who is worth all the love you can give. Not the guy who can't handle you. Not the one who only wants to see you on weekends. Not the one who tries to strip down all the things that make you who you are and replace them with things they like better.

No, the one who deserves your love might be overwhelmed by you, but they stay because they are equally captivated—they love your mind and the way your brain works, regardless of the way you look that day. They still want you, even when you're in the wrong and have done something regretful. They see you exactly the way you are and want it all, not just the parts they pick and choose; They see your worth and appreciate it.

Because that's what honest love is. And it's nothing you should be afraid of.

11

Be The Girl Who Can Love Unapologetically, Even After Her Heart Breaks

Becca Martin

Heartbreak is difficult, it's devastating and it leaves you feeling vulnerable and confused. It leaves you feeling unwanted and lost. You have to try to pull yourself together and pull your crumbling life out of the hole you've buried yourself in after the days or weeks or months of allowing yourself time to desolate and let go of the life you built with him.

Heartbreak isn't easy, it's really really tough.

I've been there, not able to eat, not able to look at anyone without bursting into tears, not moving from bed. I've felt those feelings before, but I moved on.

You have to find the broken pieces and start picking yourself up, piece by piece. You have to put yourself back together because the only way to heal is on your own by yourself. You have to mend your own heart, you have to sew it back together and care for it the way you know how.

I know you feel hurt, betrayed, wrecked and emotionally unstable. I know you've gone through hard times, spent lonely nights crying yourself to sleep and thinking it will never get better, but it will.

I promise it will.

So please, be the girl who still believes in love even after everything she has been through. After the pain and hurt you've felt and suffered, still love with all your heart when love presents itself to you again.

And when it does, promise you'll be the girl who can still love with everything she has in her because when the right guy comes along he deserves that. It will feel different and you might be holding back because you're guarding your heart, but it will be good. You might be scared, at first, but give him a chance.

He deserves the girl that isn't hung up on her ex, he deserves the girl who still wants to put everything she has into the relationship despite what she might have gone through before. He deserves your best, your everything and your undivided love because **the right guy will give that back to you.**

He will make you feel special and important. He will make you feel loved and cared for. He will make you feel like no matter what, nothing can hurt you because with him you feel safe.

Love him like you've never had a broken heart, love him like you've never felt pain, love him like he will love you. Don't hold back because you're scared of being broken and shattered again because that will only hurt your relationship. He isn't the same guy as your ex, it's a new relationship and it needs a new, fresh start. So give it the opportunity to have one.

I know you can't forget about your past, but use it to make your next relationship stronger and better.

And no matter what you do, please don't say you're giving up on love. Love is incredible and beautiful, and even though it broke your heart last time doesn't mean it will happen again.

Be the girl who still loves unapologetically even after her heart is broken because once you start holding back you're not going to feel happiness and whole again. Don't be the girl who misses on out love because of a broken heart, because **being alone is definitely not better than being in love.**

12

Please, Be This Kind Of Woman

Marisa Donnelly

Be a woman who lives honorably. Who does the right thing, even when the world isn't looking. Who treats people with love and respect, no matter where they come from, what they look like, or the stains of their past.

Be a woman isn't afraid to *be*. Who isn't afraid to feel, to be herself, to cry, to laugh, to break away from what's hurting her, or to chase things that she feels are important.

Be a woman who doesn't expect everything to be handed to her, but goes out and creates her own world. A woman who pursues her interests, chases her passions, but never steps on the beliefs of others in the process.

Be a woman who is open. Who doesn't see herself as the center of the universe, but focuses on other people. Who engages with other's thoughts and opinions. Who is continually learning.

Be a woman who is good to men. Who treats men not like steps to climb or people to provide for her, but as partners.

As equals. As beings who are just as human and broken and flawed.

Be a woman that loves. That is good to her family, her friends, her boyfriend, her husband. A woman who puts others first, who considers others feelings, who forgives and gives thanks and doesn't hold grudges.

Be a woman who laughs. Even on her broken days, even when she is tired. A woman who always finds a reason to smile.

Be a woman who treats people with respect. A woman that doesn't stand for being regarded as anything less than the treasure she is, but a woman who *is that treasure*. A woman who is kind and patient, trustworthy and respectful, giving and good—a woman who, without a doubt, *deserves* to be honored.

Be a woman who loves herself, but not more than the world. Who is strong, but not too strong that she pushes people away. Who is humble, despite her fierceness. Who stands for her rights without stepping on her male counterparts.

Be a woman who is loyal. One who doesn't lie or cheat, one who doesn't go behind her partner's back, one who doesn't deceive or break hearts, but a woman worthy of loving.

Be a woman who is imperfect, but always striving to be better. Who acknowledges her flaws and who apologizes for them. Who knows her weaknesses, but works to overcome them. Who lives a productive life, an always-improving life, a life that shines like the smile on her face.

Be a good woman, because you are. Because the world needs more like you.

13

All Women Are 'Real' Women

Rachel Yang

I'm sure a lot of us have had that "I'm not like other girls" mindset. "I like pizza and fart jokes and drinking tea," we say to ourselves. We're real.

But what is so wrong with being like other girls? Are women who don't enjoy pizza or Netflix less "real" or less complicated than others? And who determines what "real" means in the first place, and why is it such a desired trait?

Just look at the way we talk about female celebrities and you'll see that there has been an endless number of women who have been lauded for being "real" such as Emma Stone or Jennifer Lawrence, the ultimate Real Girl. People fawn over them for being different, relatable, and cool.

That's fine and dandy. But have you ever stopped to wonder why male celebrities aren't treated the same way? Yes, we drool over guys like Chris Pratt for being down to earth and funny (and hot), but don't we also celebrate men such as Zac Efron, Idris Elba, or Leonardo DiCaprio? We appreciate them for a variety of reasons, whether it's for their talent or just because they're attractive, but we still don't hold them to the same standards. They don't have to make bawdy jokes, show that they're accessible or talk about their love of junk food in order for us to love them.

We have these standards because we see men as individuals and other women as competitors.

We've been conditioned since childhood to believe that one woman's success is another woman's failure. When one woman gets the job, another doesn't. When one woman gets the guy, the other doesn't. Perhaps many of us have been in situations where we've been jealous of another woman and start to pick her apart. "I don't think she's *that* pretty," or "She's not *that smart*," are phrases that have probably slipped out of our mouths at some point.

Why do we do that to one another? When we're applying for a job, aren't we competing with *everyone,* not just other women? Why even is there this competition?

Two words: **Internalized misogyny.**

It's not really our fault. Because whether we were aware of it or not, ever since we were kids, we've been taught that being a woman is bad. We're too emotional, too superficial, and too fragile to succeed. We're not encouraged to pursue fields such as science or engineering because we can't handle it.

When little girls misbehave, they are punished for not being "ladylike." But when boys do the same, it's just "boys being boys." Has a boy ever been told what they're doing is not "gentlemanly?" Is that even a thing? (If not, can we start saying that?)

That's why to get respect, many women think they have to distance themselves from the female gender. They can't act in a way that's typically associated with being a woman. We are told that we can't enjoy healthy food or exercising as it suggests we're too focused on our weight and that's vain. We're not allowed to like makeup because that's shallow and we're insecure or hiding something. We can't like to party because it shows we're hedonistic and have no goals.

We have to be into things men like because then they'll actually respect us. We have to like video games, comic books, sex jokes, and don't forget, we can't be too emotional. Then we'll become Not Like Other Girls and be actually valued people in the eyes of men. Even many girls who do like typically "male" things are told that they're fake gamers or that they like those things to get male attention. We can't win, can we?

It's great if you actually appreciate "guy things" like video games, but why are they necessarily "guy things"? They should be everyone's things (in fact, adult women now make up the largest demographic of gamers). And why is it so bad to be into things that are typically associated with women? Is someone who likes makeup somehow less smart or "real" than you are? How do you know she's not also a book nerd who loves *Harry Potter*? So what if she's not? You cannot define someone's character by their hobbies.

There is no wrong way to be a woman. We are all real, complex, worthy people who deserve to be treated with respect. It's time we stop spending all this time tearing one another apart. That shouldn't be our goal. Instead, our goal should be to criticize and place attention on the misogynistic jerks who perpetuate stereotypical ideas about women and made us "competitors" in the first place: the YouTube video commenters whose only assessment of a woman is about whether she is "fuckable," your uncle who thinks jokes about women in kitchens are hilarious, and let's not forget, Donald Trump, whose response to a good question posed by a female journalist was that she had "blood coming out of her wherever."

These are the real villains, not other women.

14

What A Real Woman Looks Like

Ari Eastman

Real women have curves.

Real women don't.

Real women have pillowy breasts that move and dance.

Real women have mastectomies to remove cancerous cells.

Real women have skin and bones and a heart beat

and a softness

or hardness.

Real women are rough around the edges

or delicate and ethereal.

Real women have a heart that whispers with murmurs and occasional irregularities.

Real women wake up at 5 AM to feel their tennis shoes smack against pavement.

Real women wake up at 11 AM because they were up the night before

tending to families

or themselves,

learning how to love the pieces they've been told to hate.

Real women have 10 fingers.

Real women have 9 fingers.

Real women have an amputated arm.
Real women are in wheelchairs.
Real women fuck with ease.
Real women wait until marriage.
Real women believe in God
in goddesses
in a religion they find within others.
Real women spit gravel and can toss you to the wolves if you look
at them the wrong way.
Real women offer open hearts and places to rest,
places to stay until you can find something more permanent.
Real women are Bruce Jenner,
Laverne Cox
Real women overflow with love.
Real women guard their emotions,
an unopened envelope;
they do not give away their words to just anyone.
Real women read books.
Real women drink whiskey.
Real women are recovering alcoholics and work to stay that way.
Real women download Tinder because they want to hook up.
Real women download Tinder because they want real love.
Real women have plastic surgery.
Real women don't wear an ounce of makeup.

Real women get to decide
what makes them
real.

Not you.

15

To My Fellow Women: Be Whatever The Fuck You Want

Kendra Syrdal

Hey girl.

I bet you're well acquainted with all of those inspirational Pinterest quotes and Instagrams blowing up your feed about how to be a "brave woman" and that tell you to "never settle" in beautiful calligraphy laid out over a filtered sunset. I bet you see one after another and another and *another* personal essay or (god FORBID) listicle cluttering up your Facebook feed telling you how you "run the world" and how you're "strong as hell" perfectly captioned and framed with a Shutterstock image of a girl laughing.

I bet you're fully familiar with how you're supposed to be an independent, confident, never settling down or for less than what you TOTALLY deserve female. I bet you've got it. You have heard the message, you have nodded in solidarity, you have liked and Retweeted until your fingers gave out.

And you know what? I'm here to tell you one thing, and one thing only.

None of that fucking matters.

Really. Like seriously. Absolutely none of it matters. Sure, word art is fun sometimes (especially when you're decorating your bathroom) and inspirational quotes make you smile from time to time when you're absentmindedly scrolling through the interwebs. Maybe a reminder that you're a badass bitch or can do anything you put your mind to (because you are and you *can*) is nice—sure. I can roll with that. I DO roll with that.

But there is a connotation behind a lot of that Pin-spirational Porn that I simply cannot get behind, and I hope you can shrug off too.

And that's that there is a "right" way to be a woman.

See, the problem with these messages and visuals that keep flying at our faces every day is that frankly, they're no better than the Maybelline ads telling us what we *aren't* born with. They are just as influential and, potentially, just as damaging as something telling us to stick out our chests in a Bombshell Bra or telling us we're only "worth it" if we dye our hair with L'Oreal. And that's because even these supposed feminist rants that are supposed to be uplifting are in fact telling us that there is a correct way, and a *less than* correct way to conduct ourselves, carry ourselves, and ultimately look at ourselves as a woman.

They are telling us that there is only one way to woman, and it's *their* way.

And that, my fellow women, is bullshit.

It is bull with a capital B for breasts *Bullshit.*

And I for one, have had it.

I'm tired of being told that by not traveling alone across a desert I'm not brave and that by not getting a degree I don't need I'm giving up on myself. I'm tired of being told that by not waiting for someone who sweeps me off my feet I'm settling and that by not chasing a dream that's not feasibly obtainable or financially responsible I'm limiting myself.

I'm over being told that my practicality is boring and that my realistic outlook is damaging. That my sense of contentment with myself is loneliness in disguise but that my fear of dying alone is anti-feminist. That wanting kids is giving into societal pressures but NOT wanting them is failing at fulfilling some sort of duty to myself and the world.

You guys, (girls? whatever.) it's fucking *exhausting*. And I'm done trying to keep up.

Because you know what's actually damaging?

Telling other women how to live their lives simply because it doesn't align with how you've chosen to live your own.

Maybe you're a virgin but someone else practices polyamory

and multiple partners. That's DOPE. Maybe you're a stay at home mom and and someone else has had their tubes tied at 28 because they're certain they don't want kids. That's AWESOME. Maybe you're a woman who works 60 hours a week and someone else is choosing to go through all of Southeast Asia with nothing but a smartphone and a backpack. **I applaud you both.**

And I applaud you both not ONLY because you're ladies, but because you are ladies who are doing what feels right for **YOU.**

See, inspirational quotes are great. Inspirational articles are great. But they're only great if they don't make you feel bad about or make you question the life that you've chosen to live. Choosing something is not synonymous with settling. Taking a different path is not the same as limiting yourself. And living a different life than someone who looks completely opposite to you does not make you a bad woman.

Because, at the end of the day, it's nobody's life but your own.

So be whatever kind of woman you want to be.

Because I think she's pretty quotable, pretty badass, and absolutely worth writing about.

Who run the world? *You.*

You do.

So don't let anyone tell you otherwise.

16

To The Girls Who Need To Know They Deserve Better

Sierra Poston

It was great at first, being with him. You might have thought to yourself, "Wow, I found the one. This is it. This is the one that I'm going to spend the rest of my life with." Deep down in your heart, you know that something isn't right. You're happy, but you know that happiness is going to be short lived. When you're in his presence, he gives you butterflies and makes you feel giddy. It's a great feeling, but that's not how a man should make you feel. A man should make you feel protected and warm, like you know you're in good hands.

He didn't treat you the way you deserved to be treated. No one can treat someone perfectly, there will always be something they don't like. But the way he treated you was like he was taking about the garbage. Like you were a chore. He was mean, to your body and to your self-esteem. When it came to pointing out your flaws, he did a fantastic job. You weren't more than just a warm body he could sleep with. It's sad that that was all you were to him. You would have given him the world if you could, but he wouldn't have taken it because it came from you.

On some days, he would find you on his bathroom floor crying. Maybe he knew that the reason you were there was because of him, maybe he didn't, who knows? The way he looked down at you was insulting. He would ask in a disgusted tone, "Are you done yet?" How could someone you love be so degrading to your character?

You know that you deserve so much better, but you hope that he will change, that he will acknowledge your worth and start treating you the way you deserve to be treated.

You find yourself typing in the google search bar "signs of an abusive relationship." The fact that you have to google the signs of an abusive relationship should be a big enough sign for you that you are in an abusive relationship. You push that thought out of your head because you don't want to believe it. You check off the bullet points on the list in your head: critical, constant put-downs, humiliates you, insults you, controlling, denial, blame, guilt trips, excuses, refusing to communicate, provocative behavior with the opposite sex, making everything your fault, the list goes on and on. The sad thing is, you love this person, but they don't love or even respect you.

You go through all of the names he has called you with worthless, crazy, insane, and dumb being the first ones to come to mind. He calls you those names so often, you begin to think that you are in fact everything he has called you. In reality, you're priceless, reasonable, sane, and intelligent.

He will probably never change, all you can do is pray that he will treat his next girlfriend better.

You deserve to be treated so much better than what you're getting. Don't let him think that you deserve the treatment he's giving you, because you don't.

A wonderful guy will walk into your life at some point in time and you will be sitting there in awe wondering how someone so special, so perfect even, chose to be with you. He will accept you as you are and love you with all of his heart. Those are the days to look forward to.

Thought Catalog, it's a website.

www.thoughtcatalog.com

Social

facebook.com/thoughtcatalog

twitter.com/thoughtcatalog

tumblr.com/thoughtcatalog

instagram.com/thoughtcatalog

Corporate

www.thought.is

61153008R00045

Made in the USA
Lexington, KY
05 March 2017